Cocktail Parties

RECIPES

Georgeanne Brennan

GENERAL EDITOR

Chuck Williams

PHOTOGRAPHY

David Matheson

STYLING

Ben Masters

TEXT

Steve Siegelman

BONNIER
BOOKS

CONTENTS

THE ART & STYLE OF COCKTAILS

Cocktail parties are more in style than ever. Today's perfect cocktail gatherings combine the best elements of the chic affairs of the past – the colourful drinks with the exotic names, the elegance, the lively music and conversation – with a light touch, fresh global flavours, and unfussy decorative accents.

Whether it's an outdoor toast to spring, a Saturday night celebration, or an intimate fireside get-together, a cocktail party is a modern way to entertain: the length is limited to just two or three hours, most of the work can be done in advance, and the guest list can grow at the last minute because preparations are straightforward. The key to success is keeping things simple and getting the details right. Even a casual party can have flair and sophistication, as long as your vision and sense of creativity and fun come through in every element, from the food and drinks to the way you style your space.

A great cocktail party is a gift to your guests – an opportunity to see old friends and make new ones while enjoying good food and refreshing drinks. The menus, ideas, and tips in this book are designed to make giving that gift enjoyable and easy for you, with just the right balance of simple style and splashy elegance. Use them as a starting point to create the kind of cocktail party that feels right for you and your friends.

You don't need a lot of cooking or bartending experience to host a cocktail party. A little practice and you will quickly get the knack of mixing drinks and serving easy, satisfying finger foods. With this book as your guide, you will build both your confidence and your own entertaining style. Cheers!

COCKTAIL PARTY PLANNING

A cocktail party is the ideal way to celebrate a special occasion, to catch up with old friends, or to get to know new friends. The key to creating a successful event is to choose simple, stylish appetisers and drinks that can be served with ease. That is what you will find in this book: easy recipes, decorating tips, and ideas, all designed for people with busy lives and realistic budgets who want to entertain with flair.

Start with a Simple Idea

First, choose a theme, taking your cue from the occasion – a birthday, an anniversary, a new job – the season, the space, and the guests that you plan to invite. It might be a spring cocktail fête, a casual weeknight get-together, or drinks by the hearth on a chilly winter night. Use the chapters in this book for ideas as well as inspiration, and keep in mind that the theme doesn't need to be elaborate. Instead, focus on a single idea that will set the tone and tie everything together, including the invitations, guest list, decor, menu, and cocktails.

Where and When

Next, choose a location and time to match the theme. During the warmer months, if you have a garden, patio, or balcony, consider entertaining outdoors or hosting an indoor-outdoor party. Use your space creatively with an eye toward how traffic will flow from room to room. You may want to clear away or rearrange some of your furniture to accommodate more guests.

Most cocktail parties are two to three hours long. When inviting guests, use the word *cocktails* and indicate a time frame, such as six to eight o'clock, rather than only providing a start time. This will help people gauge when they can drop in and how long they should plan to stay.

Keeping It Easy

Although the words *cocktail party* once meant formal attire and opulence, today's gatherings tend to be a bit more informal and easygoing. For most parties, a buffet of appetisers and a self-service bar work quite well. Situate food and drink stations in separate areas to avoid congestion. Keep the menu and beverages uncomplicated, making them easy to prepare, restock, and serve.

Plan to serve five or six pieces of finger food per person per hour, and vary the menu to include a mix of hot and cold one- or two-bite savoury items and perhaps a dessert or two. Round out homemade offerings with quality store-bought pâtés, cheeses, cured meats, dips, nuts, and spreads. Consider hiring a helper or recruiting a friend to plate and pass appetisers, tend bar, and assist with cleanup.

BAR ESSENTIALS

For a well-outfitted home bar, stock up with the following supplies:

- Mixing glass, jigger or shot glass, and measuring spoons

- Cocktail shaker and strainer

- Bar spoon and muddler; citrus reamer, citrus stripper, and citrus zester

- Ice bucket and tongs; jugs, decanters, and punch bowl

- Small cutting board and paring knife

- Corkscrew, foil cutter, and bottle opener

- Bar towels, cocktail napkins, and coasters; straws, cocktail sticks, swizzle sticks, and decorative charms for wineglass stems

- Electric blender

EASY BAR SNACKS

Keep on hand a set of small bowls for serving the following savoury snacks:

- Crackers, breadsticks, crisps, and popcorn

- Jarred olives and spreads, such as tapenade, artichoke spread, and truffle paste; pâtés

- Nuts, such as almonds, cashews, and pistachios, and dried fruit

Setting Up the Bar

Drinks are the stars at a cocktail party, so plan to offer one or two signature cocktails and one nonalcoholic option, along with wine, beer, water, soft drinks, and a respectably stocked bar. Choose a central location for the bar, in or near the kitchen for easy access to water, ice, and refrigeration. For large parties, set up a full bar for cocktails and mixed drinks and a satellite station for self-service beverages.

Purchase party ice and store it in a cooler or in the freezer, setting some out in an ice bucket on the bar and replenishing it throughout the party. Buy more ice than you think you will need: at least 750 grams (1½ lb) per person, and more if you will be chilling glasses or bottled drinks. If making your own ice, use filtered or bottled water to avoid off flavours. Chill glasses by either filling them with ice (discard before using) or placing in the freezer for 15-30 minutes.

When purchasing alcohol and mixers, avoid very large bottles, because once they are opened, their quality deteriorates within a few weeks. Instead, buy cans, and smaller bottles, which, if unopened, will keep much longer.

Set out garnishes, such as fruit, olives, mint or other herb sprigs, citrus twists, swizzle sticks, and decorative sticks, in neatly arranged containers on the bar.

Styling the Party

Giving your party a sense of style can be remarkably easy. From decorations to lighting and music, a few simple touches can transform and focus your space. The basic principle is to create a unified look. Start by clearing away unnecessary clutter. Then choose a limited colour palette and add accents in those colours.

Flowers If possible, visit a local flower market or florist the day before your party to purchase the freshest selection of flowers and greenery. Buy most of your flowers in a single signature colour, and then add one or two complementary shades along with some greenery.

Create several arrangements and place them around the space to tie it together. Keep floral decorations for the bar and buffet low, and put them where they will not be in the way. For outdoor parties, use flowers from the garden.

Seating The less seating you have, the more your guests will be likely to mingle, so you may want to remove some furniture. Group chairs in clusters to create comfortable conversation areas, leaving plenty of room in between for people to stand and walk around. To calculate how many guests your space can accommodate, figure on about one square metre per standing person.

Lighting For indoor parties, start by dimming or turning off all overhead lighting. Illuminate the bar and food areas with lamps, and then use candles (choose dripless, unscented) as mood lighting throughout the space to create an intimate ambience. For outdoor parties, add sparkle with sturdy pillar candles with hurricane shades, oil lamps, tea lights in glasses, luminarias (votives set in paper bags, weighted with a few inches of sand), or strings of ornamental lights. Always position candles and lights at a safe distance from fabrics, plants, and other flammable objects.

Music Assemble a playlist ahead of time, so that the music matches the mood. Choose music that fits your party's theme, building from mellow selections as guests arrive to more high-energy tracks once the party is in full swing. Create some quiet conversation areas for guests who don't want to talk over the music.

Staying Organised

Cocktail parties are all about organisation and details. Start making lists early in the planning process, including a guest list, an appetizer and cocktail menu, and shopping lists. Begin planning and shopping for non-perishable items in advance. Careful preparation means you'll be more relaxed once the party begins.

Putting It All Together

If you are new to cocktail-party hosting, choose a chapter from this book and follow the work plan and recipes. Consider preparing some or all of the food at least once before the party to get a sense of how to serve and present it. Practise making the cocktails you plan to serve.

The more cocktail parties you host, the more comfortable you'll feel. As you learn what works best for your space and lifestyle, refer to this book for new ideas as well as inspiration. With the tried-and-true mix of good food, good drinks, and a spirit of fun, you'll soon discover that cocktail parties are a great way to entertain.

GLASSWARE BASICS

Only a few types of cocktail glasses are needed to serve most mixed drinks. For a typical cocktail party, plan to use at least two glasses per person.

Cocktail Glass A stemmed glass with a 125 to 180 ml (4 to 6 oz) V-shaped bowl; used for any type of cocktail.

Martini Glass A glass with a larger 180 to 250 ml (6 to 8 oz) V-shaped bowl; used for martinis and mixed drinks.

Wineglass A classic 250 to 430 ml (8 to 14 oz) stemmed tulip-shaped glass that can be used for either red or white wine.

Champagne Flute A tall, 180 to 280 ml (6 to 9 oz) tapered glass that traps the bubbles in sparkling wine.

Highball Glass A tall, 250 to 375 ml (8 to 12 oz) glass with straight sides; used for mixed drinks or blender drinks.

Old-Fashioned Glass A 160 to 310 ml (5 to 10 oz) tumbler; used for cocktails served over ice and mixed drinks.

DO-AHEAD CHECKLIST

To give yourself more time to concentrate on the food and drinks the day of the party, take care of these tasks a day ahead.

- Vacuum and dust your party space.

- Designate an area for hanging coats, such as a hall closet.

- Stock the bathroom with soap, extra towels, flowers, and candles.

- Place candles and lights around the space for illumination.

- Set out platters, serving utensils, and trays for the food.

- Place cocktail napkins and coasters at strategic locations.

- Rent or borrow extra glasses if you think you might need them and always keep some disposable glasses on hand for backup in case of breakage.

- Lay out and iron the clothes you plan to wear so you won't have to think about it at the last minute.

IMPROMPTU GATHERING

UP TO 1 WEEK IN ADVANCE

toast the nuts

UP TO 8 HOURS IN ADVANCE

make the spread and toast the
baguette slices

assemble the radishes

JUST BEFORE SERVING

prepare and assemble the antipasto plate

assemble the crostini

mix the cocktails

HOSTING AND SERVING TIPS

- Keep packaged snacks on hand for last-minute entertaining.

- Buy prepared items, such as cured meats, cheeses, stuffed peppers and vine leaves, dips, spreads, and baguettes.

- Dress up olives with lemon zest, minced fresh herbs, and extra-virgin olive oil.

- Set bread sticks out in tall glasses on the buffet and other accessible areas.

- Offer a tray of prepared cocktails, rather than taking drink orders.

- Use an assortment of plates, platters and trays, and simple decorative elements, such as candles and bowls of fruit.

DRINKS

Mango Fizz

White Lillet Cocktails

Rosemary Gin & Tonics

FOOD

Spiced Nuts

Antipasto Plate

Radishes with Butter and Sea Salt

*Crostini with Artichoke, Lemon,
and Parmesan Spread*

NATURAL SWIZZLE STICKS

For a casual gathering, using natural items such as herb sprigs and fruit segments to create cocktail stirrers lends subtle notes of freshness and spontaneity to the get-together. Choose elements that will add a complementary flavour to the drink.

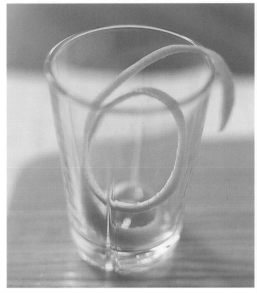

cut long spirals of orange or lemon peel using a citrus peeler. Place a spiral in a glass, draping one end over the rim, before adding ice and liquid. Serve with drinks made with citrus juice or citrus-infused spirits.

snip rosemary branches into 7.5 to 10 cm (3 to 4 inch) lengths with pruning shears. Strip off a few leaves at the base to create a handle. Serve with gin- or vodka-based drinks.

peel wedges of mango, leaving the peel attached at one end. Roll the peel back and secure with a cocktail stick or bamboo skewer. Serve with fruit- or rum-based drinks.

Mango Fizz

The tropical flavour of mango mates well with orange juice to make a base for this refreshing non-alcoholic drink. You can substitute pineapple juice for the orange juice. Add a pineapple slice as a garnish.

Select 4 tumblers or highball glasses. Fill each glass with ice. Add 6 tablespoons 60 ml (3 fl oz) of the mango nectar, 60 ml (2 fl oz) of the orange juice, and 2 tablespoons of the lime juice to each glass and stir. Top with 60 ml (2 fl oz) sparkling water. Stir, garnish each glass with a mango wedge, and serve at once.

Serves 4

Ice cubes or crushed ice

375 ml (12 fl oz) mango nectar

250 ml (8 fl oz) fresh orange juice

125 ml (4 fl oz) fresh lime juice (3-4 limes)

1 bottle (750 ml/24 fl oz) sparkling water

4 mango wedges for garnish

White Lillet Cocktails

Lillet is an aperitif made by blending white or red Bordeaux wine with orange and lemon brandies and quinine. It is wonderful served on its own, but it also makes an excellent base for a simple cocktail.

Select 4 tumblers or highball glasses. Fill each glass with ice. Add about 180 ml (6 fl oz) of the Lillet and 1 tablespoon of the Cointreau to each glass and stir. Garnish each glass with an orange strip and serve at once.

Serves 4

Ice cubes

1 bottle (750 ml/24 fl oz) white Lillet

60 ml (2 fl oz) Cointreau

4 orange peel strips, each about 6 mm ($1/4$ inch) wide and 10 cm (4 inches) long, for garnish

Rosemary Gin & Tonics

The addition of rosemary adds a refreshing twist to this classic cocktail. To release more flavour from the rosemary sprigs, squash or bruise them before putting them in the drinks.

Fill 4 tumblers or double old-fashioned glasses with ice. Add 60 ml (2 fl oz) of the gin and 180 ml (6 fl oz) of the tonic water to each glass and stir. Garnish each glass with a rosemary sprig and serve at once.

Serves 4

Ice cubes

250 ml (8 fl oz) gin

1 bottle (750 ml/24 fl oz) tonic water

4 fresh rosemary sprigs

Spiced Nuts

The combination of salt and spice always makes these seasoned nuts a hit with cocktails. Try mixing different nuts and adding other flavours such as cumin or complementary nut oils such as walnut or almond. The spiced nuts can be made a week ahead and stored in an airtight container.

Preheat the oven to 180°C (350°F).

In a bowl, combine the nuts, olive oil, salt, sugar, paprika, and cayenne and mix well. Spread the nuts in a single layer on a rimmed baking sheet. Toast, stirring several times, until the nuts are fragrant and have taken on colour, about 10 minutes. Transfer to paper towels and allow to cool, then transfer to a bowl. Garnish with the rosemary and serve at once.

Serves 8-10

500 g (1 lb) mixed shelled nuts such as almonds, walnuts, cashews, and pistachios

2 tablespoons extra-virgin olive oil

1 tablespoon sea salt

1 teaspoon sugar

2 teaspoons sweet paprika

1/2 teaspoon cayenne pepper

Rosemary leaves for garnish

Antipasto Plate

Antipasto plates are a festive and easy way to serve a crowd. Buy 500 g (1 lb) each mixed olives and assorted Italian cured meats (such as coppa, soppressata, *and salami) and some bread sticks. Arrange the olives and meats on 1 large or 2 smaller platters, leaving room for the mozzarella and mushroom appetisers below.*

Pancetta with Mozzarella

Preheat the grill. Wrap each *bocconcino* with a strip of pancetta and secure the strips with toothpicks. Place on a baking sheet, slip under the grill 10 cm (4 inches) from the heat source, and grill until the pancetta starts to crisp and the cheese is warmed through but not melted, about 4 minutes. Transfer to the platter and serve hot or warm.

1 container (375 g/12 oz) *bocconcini* (small mozzarella balls) or 250 g (¹/₂ lb) mozzarella cheese, cut into 2.5 cm (1 inch) cubes

155 g (¹/₃ lb) thinly sliced pancetta, cut into strips about 5 cm (2 inches) long and 2.5cm (1 inch) wide

Prosciutto-Stuffed Mushrooms

Preheat the oven to 180°C (350°F). Remove the mushroom stems, making a cavity in the caps. Set the caps aside. Using a sharp paring knife, trim and discard the bottom 6 mm (¹/₄ inch) of the stems. Mince the stems and set aside. Finely chop 6 of the prosciutto slices. Cut the remaining 2 slices into strips about 12 mm (¹/₂ inch) wide, then cut again into strips about 4 cm (1¹/₂ inches) long, and set aside.

In a frying pan over medium heat, melt the butter. Add the minced mushroom stems and shallots and sauté until the shallots are translucent, about 1 minute. Add the chopped prosciutto and sauté for about 30 seconds. Remove from the heat and mix in the cheese, bread crumbs, and parsley. Brush the mushroom caps with the olive oil, then stuff each cap with an equal amount of the cheese mixture and place in a lightly greased baking dish.

Bake until the mushrooms are tender and the stuffing is browned, 20-25 minutes. Let cool in the baking dish on a wire rack. To serve, roll up the prosciutto strips, place a strip on each cap, top with a parsley leaf, and arrange on the platter.

Each recipe serves 8-10

24 medium-size mushrooms

8 thin slices prosciutto, fat trimmed

4 tablespoons (60 g/2 oz) unsalted butter

60 g (2 oz) minced shallots

90 g (3 oz) soft goat cheese

20 g (²/₃ oz) store-bought or freshly made bread crumbs

2 tablespoons minced fresh flat-leaf (Italian) parsley, plus sprigs for garnish

1 tablespoon extra-virgin olive oil

2 bunches radishes with leaves
attached (18-20 radishes)

125 g (4 oz) unsalted butter,
at room temperature

3 tablespoons sea salt

RADISHES WITH BUTTER AND SEA SALT

This trio is a classic French appetiser. Oblong scarlet radishes with white tips, known as French breakfast radishes, are traditional, though any crisp, flavourful radish in any colour – red, violet, purple – will do. Serve baguette or rye bread slices alongside, if desired.

Trim the thin roots from the radishes but don't cut into the body. Remove all but a few of the youngest, smallest leaves from the tops. Cut each radish in half.

Put the butter into a ramekin just large enough to hold it, and smooth the top with a knife. Put the sea salt in a small dish.

To serve, arrange the radish halves on a platter with the butter and salt and several small butter knives.

30 baguette slices, 6 mm (1/4 inch)
thick (about 1 large baguette)

1 jar (375 g/12 oz) water-packed
artichoke hearts

1 1/2 tablespoons unsalted butter,
at room temperature

90 g (3 oz) freshly grated Parmesan
cheese

1/4 teaspoon freshly ground pepper

2 teaspoons fresh lemon juice

Salt

Finely chopped fresh flat-leaf parsley
for garnish

CROSTINI WITH ARTICHOKE, LEMON, AND PARMESAN SPREAD

Keep jars of artichoke hearts on hand in the pantry for this tasty and easy Italian-style spread. Make sure to drain and dry the artichokes well so the flavours of the spread are not diluted.

Preheat the oven to 180°C (350°F). Arrange the baguette slices in a single layer on a rimmed baking sheet. Bake until lightly golden, about 15 minutes. Turn the slices over and bake until the second side is lightly golden, about 10 minutes longer. Remove from the oven and let cool.

Drain the artichoke hearts, rinse briefly under running cold water, pat dry, and then coarsely chop. In a food processor, combine the artichoke hearts, butter, cheese, pepper, and lemon juice. Purée until smooth. Season to taste with salt.

Evenly spread the purée on the baguette slices. Arrange the crostini on a platter, garnish with the chopped parsley, and serve.

Each recipe serves 8-10

SPRING COCKTAIL FÊTE

HOSTING AND SERVING TIPS

- The day before the party, watch the path of the sun to determine where to set up the bar, buffet, and seating.

- Position the buffet table and bar near the entrance to the house for easy cleanup and maintenance.

- Set out sunscreen, sun hats, and insect repellent for guests to use.

- Use strings of brightly coloured paper lanterns as decorative accents even for daytime parties.

- Plan your decorating around the setting's flowers and foliage. Bring in potted flowering plants for extra colour.

DRINKS

Cherry Sparklers

Strawberry Daiquiris

Mojitos

FOOD

Smoked Salmon and Watercress Wraps

Bite-Sized Leek Tartlets

*Endive Tipped with Ahi and
Green Peppercorns*

Asparagus with Parmesan Dipping Sauce

WORK PLAN

UP TO 12 HOURS IN ADVANCE
bake the tartlet shells

UP TO 8 HOURS IN ADVANCE
roast the asparagus

UP TO 4 HOURS IN ADVANCE
assemble the endive with ahi
make the Parmesan dipping sauce

JUST BEFORE SERVING
assemble the asparagus and dipping sauce
mix the filling and bake the tartlets
assemble the salmon and watercress wraps
mix the cocktails

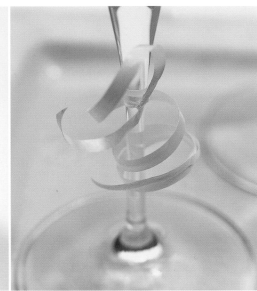

cut a 10 cm (4 inch) length of thin curling ribbon and tie one end to a bamboo skewer, decorative stick, or swizzle stick. Use scissors to curl the ribbon.

tie a 15 cm (6 inch) length of curling ribbon around the stem of a martini glass, wineglass, Champagne flute, or other stemware. Once the ribbon is in place, curl it.

wrap a 30 to 60 cm (12 to 24 inch) length of raffia or ribbon around the base of a tall glass and secure with a knot. If desired, wrap a leaf around the glass first and use the raffia to hold it in place.

GLASSWARE FLOURISHES

Once you have finished decorating your party space, extend the festive spirit by decorating your cocktail glasses. Simple accents can make even everyday glasses more celebratory and can reinforce your theme and colour palette. Curling ribbon, raffia, and bamboo skewers are all you need to get started.

CHERRY SPARKLERS

These colourful drinks capture the taste of spring. If you have a juice press, make your own cherry juice. Otherwise, purchase high-quality bottled juice. You can adjust the amount of sparkling water to your guests' tastes.

Select 4 large cocktail or highball glasses. Put several ice cubes in each glass. Pour 180 ml (6 fl oz) of the cherry juice over the ice in each glass, and then top with about 60 ml (2 fl oz) of the sparkling water. Garnish each glass with a cherry and serve at once.

Serves 4

Ice cubes

750 ml (24 fl oz) cherry juice, preferably fresh

1 bottle (750 ml/24 fl oz) sparkling water

4 fresh cherries with stems intact for garnish

STRAWBERRY DAIQUIRIS

Smooth, fruity, and refreshing, these daiquiris taste as good as they look. For a creamier taste, top each drink with freshly whipped cream before garnishing with a strawberry half.

Select 4 cocktail glasses. In a blender, combine the strawberry purée, rum, sugar, and lime juice. Add ice to cover by 4 cm (1½ inches) and process until liquefied. Pour into the glasses and garnish each glass with a strawberry half, resting it on the rim. Serve at once.

Serves 4

180 ml (6 fl oz) puréed sweetened frozen strawberries

250 ml (8 fl oz) light rum

4 teaspoons sugar

Juice of 4 limes

Ice cubes

2 strawberries with hulls intact, halved lengthwise, for garnish

MOJITOS

Originating in Cuba, the mojito *has a fresh, sweet-crisp taste that comes from the perfect marriage of lime, sugar, and mint. Muddling, or crushing, the ingredients together is a key step in achieving this balance. If you don't have a muddler, use the handle of a wooden spoon.*

Select 4 tall or highball glasses. Put 8 of the mint sprigs, 1 tablespoon of the sugar, and the juice of 1 lime in each glass. Muddle to bruise, but not pulverize, the mint. Add some ice and 60 ml (2 fl oz) of the rum to each glass. Top each glass with sparkling water, stir well, and serve at once.

Serves 4

32 fresh mint sprigs

4 tablespoons (50g /1³/₄ oz) superfine (caster) sugar

Juice of 4 limes

Ice cubes

250 ml (8 fl oz) light rum

1 bottle (750 ml /24 fl oz) sparkling water

SMOKED SALMON AND WATERCRESS WRAPS

Savoury smoked salmon and crisp watercress are often partnered, but wrapping them with herbed goat cheese and then serving them in bite-sized spirals makes for a fresh presentation. For a milder taste, substitute cream cheese for the goat cheese.

In a bowl, mix together the goat cheese and half-and-half until the mixture has a smooth, spreadable consistency. Spread each tortilla with one-third of the cheese mixture, covering the entire surface. Place one-third of the salmon strips on top of the cheese and top with one-third of the watercress leaves. Roll up each tortilla into a snug cylinder and place, seam side down, on a cutting board. Using a serrated knife, cut crosswise into slices about 2.5 cm (1 inch) wide. Arrange the slices on a platter, garnish with the watercress sprigs, and serve.

Serves 12-14

90 g (3 oz) herbed fresh goat cheese, at room temperature

3 tablespoons half-and-half (half whole milk and half single cream)

3 large flour tortillas

155 g (5 oz) sliced smoked salmon, cut into strips 2.5 cm (1 inch) wide

Leaves from 2 bunches watercress, tough stems removed (30 g /1 oz leaves), plus sprigs for garnish

Bite-Sized Leek Tartlets

Use the ready-to-roll pastry available at supermarkets to make the pastry shells. They can be baked up to 12 hours in advance.

Preheat the oven to 200°C (400°F). Have ready mini-muffin pans with 24 cups. Using a 5 cm (2 inch) round pastry cutter, cut out 24 pastry rounds, reserving any extra dough. Fit a round into each muffin cup. To keep the pastry flat while baking, make a loose ball of aluminium foil and place into each cup and bake for 4 minutes. Remove the foil, prick each pastry shell with fork tines, and continue to bake until golden, 2-3 minutes longer. Repeat the process with the remaining dough (you should have a total of at least 36 rounds). Allow to cool completely on wire racks. Reduce the oven temperature to 180°C (350°F).

In a frying pan over medium heat, melt the butter. Add the leek and cook, stirring, until softened, about 15 minutes. Cover, reduce the heat to low, and cook until translucent, 5-7 minutes longer. Set aside.

In a bowl, whisk together the eggs, cream, salt, pepper, and nutmeg. Whisk in the leek mixture, then spoon into the cooled pastry shells, filling to the brim. Bake until puffed and lightly golden, 10-12 minutes. Let cool in the pans on a wire rack. Serve warm or at room temperature.

3 rolls store-bought shortcrust pastry dough, each about 33 cm (13 inches) in diameter and 6 mm (^{1}/4 inch) thick, thawed in the refrigerator

2 tablespoons unsalted butter

1 large leek, white part only, minced

3 large eggs, at room temperature

430 ml (14 fl oz) double cream

^{1}/2 teaspoon salt

^{1}/4 teaspoon ground white pepper

^{1}/8 teaspoon freshly grated nutmeg

Endive Tipped with Ahi and Green Peppercorns

Delicate leaves of Belgian endive, just slightly bitter, are elegant carriers for diced tuna, cream cheese, and tart green peppercorns.

Cut off 12 mm (^{1}/2 inch) from the stem end of each endive. Separate the leaves, then choose the 40 largest leaves (reserve the others for another use). Spread about 1^1/2 teaspoons of cream cheese at the base end of each leaf, covering one-fourth of the leaf. Sprinkle with about 1 teaspoon tuna and a few of the peppercorns. Cover and refrigerate until serving. They will keep for up to 4 hours.

Each recipe serves 12-14

5 heads Belgian endive (chicory)

1 pack (250 g/8 oz) cream cheese, at room temperature

500 g (1 lb) sashimi-grade ahi tuna, finely diced

75 g (2^1/2 oz) pickled green peppercorns, rinsed and patted dry

Asparagus with Parmesan Dipping Sauce

48 asparagus spears, ends trimmed

90 ml (3 fl oz) balsamic vinegar

60 ml (2 fl oz) extra-virgin olive oil

1 teaspoon salt

1 teaspoon freshly ground pepper

DIPPING SAUCE

125 g (¼ lb) freshly grated Parmesan cheese

2 tablespoons extra-virgin olive oil

60 g (2 oz) plain yogurt

2 tablespoons minced fresh flat-leaf (Italian) parsley

Salt and freshly ground pepper

Roasting caramelises the natural sugars in the asparagus, enhancing their flavour. The asparagus can be cooked up to 8 hours in advance, and the dipping sauce can be made up to 4 hours in advance. Cover and refrigerate separately and bring to room temperature before serving.

Preheat the oven to 230°C (450°F).

Arrange the asparagus spears in a single layer in 2 shallow baking dishes. Drizzle with the vinegar and olive oil, then sprinkle with the salt and pepper. Turn several times to coat the spears well. Roast, turning several times, until tender but crisp and the tips are lightly golden, 10-15 minutes. Transfer to a platter.

To make the dipping sauce, in a small bowl, whisk together the cheese, olive oil, yogurt, and parsley. Whisk in salt and pepper to taste.

Transfer the sauce to a serving bowl and place alongside the platter of asparagus. Serve at room temperature.

Serves 12-14

SATURDAY NIGHT

HOSTING AND SERVING TIPS

- Organise early: write lists, shop, and make a party plan at least two weeks ahead of time.

- Serve drinks made in a cocktail shaker in cocktail glasses that are chilled.

- Use silver, stainless-steel, chrome, and glass serving pieces.

- Present finger food and cocktails on trays and platters with linens in neutral tones, so the colours stand out.

- Use cloth cocktail napkins rather than paper for a more refined look.

- Create a sparkling effect by clustering pillar candles of various heights on the mantel or around the room.

DRINKS

Apricot Froths

Meyer Lemon Drops

Classic Cosmopolitans

Blood Orange Cosmopolitans

FOOD

Spicy Hoummus with Flat Bread Crisps

Toasts with Goat Cheese, Walnuts, and Honey

Ham and Gorgonzola Panini

Radicchio Cups with Smoked Trout

Lamb and Sweet Pepper Kebabs

Italian Ice Cream Cones

WORK PLAN

UP TO 3 DAYS IN ADVANCE
make the hoummus

UP TO 1 DAY IN ADVANCE
toast the pitta
make the apricot purée

UP TO 4 HOURS IN ADVANCE
assemble the panini
marinate the lamb kebabs

JUST BEFORE SERVING
assemble the toasts and radicchio cups
grill the kebabs
bake the panini
prepare the ice cream cones
mix the cocktails

cut strips of lemon peel using a vegetable peeler or citrus peeler, curl them into tight balls, and secure each with a cocktail stick. Use with citrus-spiked cocktails.

cube fresh apricots, peaches, or nectarines and thread two cubes onto each cocktail stick. Just before serving, roll each stick in sugar, and then balance on the rim of the glass. Use with fruity blender drinks and punches.

peel and segment a blood orange with a sharp paring knife. Spear each segment onto a cocktail stick. Use with drinks made with orange juice or orange liqueur.

EASY GARNISHES

From the glass to the garnish, cocktails are all about presentation. Garnishes don't have to be elaborate or time-consuming to add a note of colour and sophistication. Make these simple garnishes ahead of time and store them, covered with a damp paper towel, in the refrigerator.

APRICOT FROTHS

You can use either fresh apricots or purchase apricot purée to make this simple yet satisfying drink. If desired, it can be made in a big batch for serving from a punch bowl. Topping off the glasses with sparkling water ensures a frothy crown. The purée can be made a day ahead, covered, and refrigerated.

4 ripe apricots, halved and pitted, or 125 ml (4 fl oz) apricot purée

90 ml (3 fl oz) water

2 tablespoons sugar

Ice cubes

1 bottle (750 ml/24 fl oz) sparkling water, chilled

8 apricot cubes for garnish

Select 4 cocktail glasses. If using fresh apricots, place them in a small saucepan, add the water and 2 tablespoons sugar, and bring to a boil over medium-high heat. Cook, stirring occasionally, until soft, about 4 minutes. Remove from the heat and allow to cool. If using apricot purée, add the water and only 1 tablespoon of the sugar and stir until the sugar dissolves.

Transfer the cooked apricots to a blender and process until smooth. Or, pour the purée into the blender. Add ice to cover by 4 cm (1¹/₂ inches) and process until liquefied. Divide evenly among the glasses and top with sparkling water. Garnish each glass with 2 apricot cubes speared on a cocktail stick. Serve at once.

Serves 4

MEYER LEMON DROPS

This chic cocktail is elevated by using Meyer lemon vodka, made with prized sweet Meyer lemons. If you cannot find it, you can use any type of citrus-infused vodka.

1 tablespoon granulated sugar

1 lemon wedge

Ice cubes

250 ml (8 fl oz) Meyer lemon vodka

60 ml (2 fl oz) triple sec

4 lemon peel strips, each curled tightly into a ball for garnish

Select 4 martini glasses. Spread the sugar on a small plate. Rub the outside rim of each glass with the lemon wedge. Holding a glass at an angle, roll the outside rim in the sugar. Repeat with the other 3 glasses. Put the glasses in the freezer to chill for at least 30 minutes.

Fill a tall cocktail shaker half full with ice. Add the vodka and triple sec. Cover with the lid and shake for 20 seconds, then strain into the chilled glasses. Garnish each glass with a lemon strip and serve at once.

Serves 4

Classic Cosmopolitans

Ice cubes

250 ml (8 fl oz) citrus vodka

60 ml (2 fl oz) triple sec

60 ml (2 fl oz) cranberry juice

60 ml (2 fl oz) fresh lime juice

4 fresh cherries for garnish

4 lime twists for garnish

Although the cosmopolitan, popularly known as the cosmo, is a relative youngster in the history of cocktails, it has become a staple at bars and parties. Its signature red colour comes from the addition of cranberry juice. For a paler version, reduce the amount to a few drops per drink.

Chill 4 martini glasses. Fill a tall cocktail shaker half full with ice. Pour in the vodka, triple sec, cranberry juice, and lime juice. Cover with the lid and shake for 20 seconds, then strain into the chilled glasses. Garnish each glass with a cherry and a lime twist speared on a cocktail stick. Serve at once.

Serves 4

Blood Orange Cosmopolitans

Ice cubes

250 ml (8 fl oz) orange vodka

60 ml (2 fl oz) triple sec

60 ml (2 fl oz) fresh blood orange juice

60 ml (2 fl oz) fresh lime juice

4 blood orange segments for garnish

In this aromatic and sophisticated variation on the classic, the cosmopolitan sheds its usual cranberry juice for the fragrant, scarlet juice of the blood orange.

Chill 4 martini glasses. Fill a tall cocktail shaker half full with ice. Pour in the vodka, triple sec, orange juice, and lime juice. Cover with the lid and shake for 20 seconds, then strain into the chilled glasses. Garnish each glass with a blood orange segment speared on a cocktail stick. Serve at once.

Serves 4

Spicy Houmous with Flat Bread Crisps

Houmous can be quickly made with just a few items that can be kept on hand. Adjust the taste by using hot paprika or using more or less garlic or lemon juice, or by adding a little cumin. You can make the houmous up to 3 days in advance and toast the pitta up to a day ahead.

Preheat the oven to 180°C (350°F). Using kitchen scissors or a sharp knife, cut each pitta into strips 2.5 cm (1 inch) wide, then cut the strips into 2.5 cm (1 inch) pieces. Arrange the pitta pieces in a single layer on a rimmed baking sheet. Bake until lightly golden, about 10 minutes. Remove from the oven, let cool, and set aside.

In a food processor, combine the chickpeas, lemon juice, salt, paprika, cayenne, garlic, and olive oil and process until puréed, about 5 minutes. Spoon into a serving bowl, sprinkle with the parsley, and serve with the pitta crisps.

Serves 14-16

4 pitta bread rounds

1 can (780 g /25 oz) chickpeas (garbanzo beans), drained and rinsed

Juice of 3 lemons

1 teaspoon salt

1 teaspoon mild paprika

$1/4$ teaspoon cayenne pepper

1 clove garlic, minced

60 ml (2 fl oz) extra-virgin olive oil

10 g ($1/3$ oz) minced fresh flat-leaf (Italian) parsley

Toasts with Goat Cheese, Walnuts, and Honey

Sweet honey and savoury walnuts make excellent accompaniments to the goat cheese in this easy-to-make finger food. You can toast the baguette slices up to 8 hours in advance and then top them at the last minute.

Preheat the oven to 180°C (350°F). Arrange the baguette slices in a single layer on a rimmed baking sheet. Bake until lightly golden, about 15 minutes. Turn the slices over and bake until the second side is lightly golden, about 10 minutes longer. Remove from the oven, allow to cool, and set aside.

Spread each toast with about 2 teaspoons of the goat cheese. Drizzle each with a generous $1/2$ teaspoon of the honey and sprinkle with a generous 1 teaspoon of the walnuts. Serve at once.

Serves 14-16

40 baguette slices, 6 mm ($1/4$ inch) thick (about $1 1/2$ baguettes)

250 g ($1/2$ lb) soft goat cheese

185 g (6 oz) honey

125 g (4 oz) chopped walnuts

Ham and Gorgonzola Panini

These panini are made with fluffy focaccia that is filled, heated, and then cut into small pieces. They can be prepared up to 4 hours in advance, wrapped tightly in aluminium foil, and set aside until heating.

20 cm (8 inch) square focaccia, about 315-375 g (10-12 oz) and 4 cm (1½ inches) thick

155 g (⅓ lb) creamy Gorgonzola cheese, at room temperature

1½ tablespoons double cream

1½ tablespoons extra-virgin olive oil

125 g (¼ lb) thinly sliced ham

Preheat the oven to 180°C (350°F). Cut the focaccia in half horizontally, yielding 2 pieces each about 2 cm (¾ inch) thick.

In a small bowl, stir together the cheese and cream to make a spreadable paste. Place the focaccia pieces, cut side up, on a flat work surface. Drizzle 1 piece with half of the olive oil and then spread with the cheese mixture and top with the ham. Drizzle the other focaccia piece with the remaining olive oil and place, oil side down, on top of the ham. Using your hands, gently press down on the top. Wrap tightly in aluminium foil, place in the oven, and bake until the cheese melts, about 20 minutes.

Remove from the oven, unwrap, and cut into 4 strips each about 5 cm (2 inches) wide. Cut the strips crosswise into 2.5 cm (1 inch) pieces and arrange on a platter. Serve at once.

Radicchio Cups with Smoked Trout

The eye-catching white and magenta of radicchio add a fanciful note to any cocktail gathering, and using the leaves as cups yields a bite-sized hors d'oeuvre. For a variation, substitute smoked salmon or whitefish or chopped raw sashimi-grade ahi tuna for the trout.

1 head radicchio, cored

125 g (4 oz) crème fraîche

250-375 g (½-¾ lb) smoked trout fillet, broken into bite-sized pieces

Juice of 1 lemon

15 g (½ oz) minced fresh dill

Thin lemon slices, halved, for garnish

Separate the radicchio leaves. Cut the large leaves into 2 or 3 pieces. Leave the smaller leaves whole.

At the base of each leaf, put about 1 teaspoon of crème fraîche and a piece or two of trout. Drizzle with the lemon juice and sprinkle with the dill. Arrange on a platter, garnish with the lemon slices, and serve.

Each recipe serves 14-16

LAMB AND SWEET PEPPER KEBABS

Kebabs are always welcome party fare. Here, they are threaded with lamb, rather than the more common chicken or pork, and bright red peppers. The garlicky marinade helps keep the lamb moist as it cooks and adds a burst of flavour. If you use lamb shoulder, select the leanest piece you can find, or buy a little extra and trim away any excess fat.

In a large bowl, stir together the olive oil, garlic, oregano, salt, black pepper, and red pepper flakes. Add the lamb and red peppers and turn to coat evenly. Cover and marinate for 1 hour at room temperature or 4 hours in the refrigerator. Soak the kebab skewers in water for 30 minutes.

Preheat the grill. Remove the lamb and red peppers from the marinade, discarding the marinade. Drain the kebab skewers and carefully thread 3 or 4 lamb pieces alternating with the pepper pieces onto each skewer.

Arrange the kebabs in a single layer on a rimmed baking sheet. Slip under the grill 10 cm (4 inches) from the heat source and grill until sizzling and brown, 12-14 minutes. Turn the kebabs and grill until the second side is browned, about 5 minutes longer. Transfer the kebabs to a warmed platter, garnish with the lime wedges, if using, and serve hot or warm.

Serves 14-16

60 ml (2 fl oz) extra-virgin olive oil

3 cloves garlic, crushed

1 teaspoon dried oregano

1/2 teaspoon salt

1/2 teaspoon freshly ground black pepper

1/2 teaspoon red pepper flakes

1 kg (2 lb) boneless lamb shoulder or leg, cut into 4 cm (1 1/2 inch) cubes

2 red peppers (capsicums), seeded and cut into 2.5 cm (1 inch) pieces

18 wooden bamboo kebab skewers

Grilled lime wedges for garnish (optional)

ITALIAN ICE CREAM CONES

Cocktail parties are about having fun, and what could be more fun than an ice cream cone for dessert? Ice cream and sorbet come in many flavours, making this a good way to please friends with a variety of different favourites. Visit an ice cream shop where you can taste the flavours, then select what you like best.

2 litres (4 pints) chocolate, vanilla, strawberry, or pistachio ice cream or lemon, lime, or raspberry sorbet, or a combination

20 mini ice cream cones

20 store-bought tuile biscuits or wafers

To make the ice cream and/or sorbet easier to scoop, remove from the freezer and put on the worktop for about 10 minutes to soften slightly. Using a small ice-cream scoop (about 4.5 cm/$1^{3}/_{4}$ inches across the top) or a sturdy tablespoon, fill each cone with a scoop of ice cream or sorbet. If you have small ice-cream parlour spoons, stand a spoon in the side of each scoop, and then stick a tuile biscuit in the top. If desired, slip a paper doily around each ice cream cone, and then serve at once, providing small napkins to catch any drips.

Serves 14-16

AL FRESCO

WORK PLAN

UP TO 4 HOURS IN ADVANCE

make the cocktail sauce

marinate the calamari

toast the baguette slices

UP TO 2 HOURS IN ADVANCE

assemble the cucumber with fresh crab

make the broad bean purée

JUST BEFORE SERVING

grill the calamari kebabs

assemble the crostini and
prawn cocktails

mix the cocktails

HOSTING AND
SERVING TIPS

- Put seat cushions or pillows on benches, ledges, and folding chairs for more comfortable seating.

- Set out oil lamps or candles in hurricane lamps, with matches alongside, to illuminate as the sun sets.

- Decorate the party space, food platters, trays, and drinks with flowers.

- Brighten nonflowering plants by adorning them with hearty cut flowers that will stay fresh for a few hours.

- Float flowers in glass bowls filled with water for simple centrepieces.

- Check the weather forecast a day ahead and have a backup plan for moving the party indoors.

DRINKS

Watermelon Refreshers

Margaritas

Tequila Sunrises

FOOD

Grilled Calamari Kebabs

Prawn Cocktails

Cucumber with Fresh Crab

Crostini with Broad Bean Spread and Mint

FRUITFUL ICE CUBES

Decorative ice cubes are easy to make and add both colour and flavour. Place citrus wedges or zest or melon balls in ice cube trays, fill with water, and freeze. Filtered or bottled water will give you the clearest cubes. For an even more festive look, use novelty trays in decorative shapes, such as stars and moons.

peel and segment lemons with a paring knife. Place the segments in ice cube trays, leaving a little of each segment exposed. Fill with water and freeze. Use with drinks that include lemon or other citrus juice.

cut long shreds of lime, lemon, or orange zest, or a mixture. Arrange a few shreds of zest in ice cube trays, fill with water, and freeze. Use in margaritas and other citrus-accented drinks.

scoop balls of watermelon, cantaloupe, or other type of melon. Place the balls in ice cube trays, fill with water, and freeze. Use in tropical-themed drinks or in drinks made with melon or a melon-flavoured liqueur.

WATERMELON REFRESHERS

Watermelons, with their high water content, are a natural base for a refreshing drink. A yellow seedless watermelon can be substituted for the red watermelon, for an equally refreshing sunny yellow cool drink.

Select 4 tumblers or old-fashioned glasses. In a blender, combine half of the watermelon flesh (reserve the remaining flesh for ice cubes, page 71), the ice, and the lime juice and purée until smooth. Divide the purée evenly among the glasses. Garnish each glass with a mint sprig.

Serves 4

1 small red seedless watermelon, about 1.25 kg (2^1/$_2$ lb), rind removed

250 ml (8 fl oz) crushed ice

2 tablespoons fresh lime juice (1-2 limes)

4 fresh mint sprigs for garnish

MARGARITAS

Not only are margaritas the quintessential party drink, but they are also easy to make. Using sea salt gives the cocktail extra texture along with its signature salty taste. Be careful to salt only the outside rim of the glass.

Select 4 tumblers or old-fashioned glasses. On a small plate, stir together the salt and lime zest. Rub the outside rim of each glass with the lime wedge. Holding a glass at an angle, roll the outside rim in the salt mixture. Repeat with the other 3 glasses. Fill each glass with ice and 2 or 3 lime slices, if desired.

Fill a cocktail shaker half full with ice. Add the tequila, Cointreau, and lime juice. Cover with the lid and shake for 20 seconds. Strain into the glasses, garnish each glass with a lime slice, and serve at once.

Serves 4

1 tablespoon sea salt

1 teaspoon grated lime zest

1 lime wedge

Ice cubes

8-12 thin lime slices (optional), plus 4 thin lime slices for garnish

250 ml (8 fl oz) tequila

125 ml (4 fl oz) Cointreau or triple sec

125 ml (4 fl oz) fresh lime juice (3-4 limes)

Tequila Sunrises

The quality of this popular drink depends in large part on the quality of the orange juice. That means always using freshly squeezed juice. For a more vibrantly coloured drink, squeeze the juice of blood oranges. Increase the grenadine to 60 ml (2 fl oz) for a sweeter drink.

Select 4 highball glasses. On a plate, stir together the sugar and the zest. Rub the outside rim of each glass with an orange wedge. Holding a glass at an angle, roll the outside rim in the sugar mixture. Repeat with the other 3 glasses. Fill each glass with ice. Add 60 ml (2 fl oz) of the tequila, 125 ml (4 fl oz) of the orange juice, and $1^{1}/_{2}$ teaspoons of the grenadine to each glass. Allow the grenadine to settle to the bottom of the glasses. Garnish each glass with an orange slice and serve at once.

Serves 4

1 tablespoon granulated sugar

1 tablespoon grated orange zest

1 or 2 orange wedges

Ice cubes

250 ml (8 fl oz) silver tequila

500 ml (16 fl oz) fresh orange juice

2 tablespoons grenadine

4 thin orange slices for garnish

Grilled Calamari Kebabs

Calamari, or squid, can be found in the frozen fish section of many markets, making it easy to prepare these simple appetizers. If you can't find full bodies, use calamari rings and thread several onto each skewer.

In a shallow baking dish, whisk together the soy sauce, wine, garlic, ginger, and brown sugar until the sugar dissolves. Rinse the calamari bodies and pat dry with paper towels. Cut the bodies in half lengthwise, add to the dish, and turn to coat well. Cover and refrigerate for at least 1 hour or up to 4 hours. Soak the skewers in water for at least 30 minutes.

Prepare a charcoal or gas grill for direct grilling over high heat. Lightly oil the grill rack and a grill basket. Drain the skewers and carefully thread the calamari onto them, discarding the marinade. Arrange as many kebabs as will fit side by side in the grill basket and place on the grill rack. Grill, turning once, until the calamari are opaque throughout, about 2 minutes on each side. Transfer to a platter and repeat with the remaining kebabs. Serve hot or warm.

Serves 10-12

3 tablespoons soy sauce

1 tablespoon dry red wine

2 cloves garlic, crushed

2 teaspoons peeled and grated fresh ginger

1 teaspoon firmly packed light brown sugar

750 g ($1^{1}/_{2}$ lb) cleaned calamari bodies

36 wooden bamboo skewers

PRAWN COCKTAILS

Seafood aficionados tend to love prawn cocktail. In this version, the prawns are served in cocktail glasses on a bed of shredded lettuce, making them easy to eat at a cocktail party. For a milder sauce, reduce the amount of chilli sauce.

In a bowl, stir together the ketchup, chilli sauce, lemon juice, Worcester sauce, and vinegar and mix well. Set the sauce aside.

Select 12 glasses, such as cocktail glasses or short water glasses. Shred the romaine and divide among the glasses, making a bed in each. Put 4 of the prawns in each glass and top with about 2 tablespoons of the sauce. Stick a celery stalk, base down, into each glass. Cut a slit in each lemon slice half, slip onto each glass rim, and serve at once.

Serves 12

345 ml (11 fl oz) ketchup

3 tablespoons Thai chilli sauce

2 tablespoons fresh lemon juice

2 teaspoons *each* Worcester sauce and red wine vinegar

12 romaine or cos lettuce leaves

48 cooked and peeled prawns with tail segments intact about 1 kg (2 lb)

12 pale inner celery ribs with leaves

6 thin lemon slices, halved, for garnish

CUCUMBER WITH FRESH CRAB

Here, thin slices of cucumber replace the typical biscuits, delivering a fresh flavour and crunchy texture that complements the sweet-tasting crab. Olive oil-packed canned tuna or cooked chicken would make a fine substitute for the crab.

Peel 5 of the cucumbers and cut into slices 6 mm (¼ inch) thick. You should have 48 slices. Peel, halve, seed, and mince the remaining cucumber. Set aside.

In a bowl, combine the mayonnaise, olive oil, lemon juice, shallots, tarragon, salt, and cayenne and mix well. Add the crabmeat and turn gently with a fork to mix, being careful not to break up the crabmeat. Put about 1½ teaspoons of the crab mixture on each cucumber slice and top with a little of the minced cucumber.

Arrange on a platter, cover, and refrigerate for up to 2 hours before serving.

Serves 10-12

6 cucumbers

3½ tablespoons mayonnaise

1 teaspoon extra-virgin olive oil

1½ teaspoons fresh lemon juice

4 teaspoons minced shallots

2 teaspoons minced fresh tarragon

¼ teaspoon salt

¼ teaspoon cayenne pepper

280 g (9 oz) fresh-cooked crabmeat, chilled and picked over for shell fragments

Crostini with Broad Bean Spread and Mint

30 baguette slices, 6 mm (¼ inch) thick (about 1 large baguette)

1 kg (2 lb) broad beans

3 tablespoons extra-virgin olive oil, plus extra for drizzling

6 tablespoons (90 ml/ 3 fl oz) double cream

2 teaspoons sea salt

1 teaspoon freshly ground pepper

3 tablespoons minced fresh mint

30 small fresh mint sprigs for garnish

Fresh broad beans have a meaty, earthy taste that is highly valued around the Mediterranean. The larger, more mature beans make an exceptional spread and combine well with fresh herbs. Here mint is used, but chives or tarragon can be used in its place.

Preheat the oven to 180°C (350°F).

Arrange the baguette slices in a single layer on a rimmed baking sheet. Bake until lightly golden, about 15 minutes. Turn the slices over and bake until the second side is lightly golden, about 10 minutes longer. Remove from the oven, allow to cool, and set aside.

Remove the broad beans from their pods and discard the pods. Bring a pot three-quarters full of water to a boil over high heat. Add the broad beans and cook until the beans are tender and the skins slip easily from the beans, 10-25 minutes; the timing depends on the age of the beans. Drain the beans in a colander and, when cool enough to handle, slip off the skins and discard them.

In a food processor, combine the beans, the 3 tablespoons olive oil, 3 tablespoons of the cream, the salt, the pepper, and the minced mint and process until a creamy purée forms. If the mixture seems too dry, add up to 3 tablespoons more cream. Taste and adjust the seasoning. (The purée may be made up to 2 hours in advance, covered, and refrigerated; bring to room temperature before spreading on the baguette slices.)

Spread the purée on the baguette slices and arrange on a platter. Garnish the crostini with the mint sprigs and then drizzle them with olive oil. Serve at once.

Serves 10-12

SUMMER COCKTAILS

HOSTING AND
SERVING TIPS

- Decorate the table with fresh flowers and citrus fruits and leaves.

- Store the ice cooler in a shady spot, and perishable food out of the sun.

- Serve mostly room-temperature food to cut down on kitchen time.

- Use good china and glassware to create a cocktail-party atmosphere.

- Serve an alcoholic punch drink to lighten bartending duties.

DRINKS

Cucumber-Lime Cocktail

Citrus Caipirinhas

Sangria

Peach Bellini

FOOD

Figs Wrapped in Prosciutto

Bite-Sized Courgette Frittata

Beef Tenderloin Canapés with
Chopped Vine Tomatoes

White and Yellow Corn Fritters with
Romesco Sauce

Fold-up Blueberry and Raspberry Fruit Tarts

WORK PLAN

UP TO 1 WEEK IN ADVANCE

make the *romesco* sauce

UP TO 6 HOURS IN ADVANCE

assemble the figs and prosciutto

toast the baguette slices

UP TO 2 HOURS IN ADVANCE

roast the beef tenderloin

make the frittata

make the corn fritters

mix the berries for the tarts

JUST BEFORE SERVING

assemble the beef tenderloin canapés

bake the berry tarts

mix the cocktails

slice lemons and navel oranges into half or quarter rounds. Remove any seeds from the citrus slices. Or, slice limes or other fruits in contrasting colours.

layer the citrus slices in the bottom of each glass, stacking them in a pleasing pattern of alternating colours.

fill the glasses with filtered or bottled water to cover the slices and place in the freezer to freeze. Pour cocktails into the frozen glasses just before serving.

CITRUS DRINK COOLER

Freezing water and citrus slices in the bottom of a glass is a clever way to create a colourful effect. Use sturdy, freezer-safe glasses, preferably with a distinctively shaped base. For the prettiest effect, choose citrus and drinks with contrasting colours.

Cucumber-Lime Cocktail

In the heat of summer, this refreshing non-alcoholic drink is guaranteed to cool you down. You will need 6 or 7 large limes for both the juice and the garnish. If possible, use a mandoline to cut the cucumber and lime slices, which will give you thin, uniform slices.

Select 4 old-fashioned or short glasses. Combine 60 ml (2 fl oz) of the lime juice and $1^1/2$ tablespoons of sugar in each glass and stir to dissolve the sugar. Fill the glasses with ice and then top each glass with 180 ml (6 fl oz) of the sparkling water. Garnish each glass with several cucumber and lime slices and serve at once.

Serves 4

250 ml (8 fl oz) fresh lime juice, (4-5 large limes)

6 tablespoons superfine (caster) sugar

Ice cubes

750 ml (24 fl oz) sparkling water, chilled

Thin cucumber and lime slices for garnish

Citrus Caipirinhas

Caipirinha, *the national drink of Brazil, is classically made with* cachaça, *a sugarcane brandy, and lime. This version, with lemon, is a little tangier. If you prefer lime, use 1 lime for each glass, cutting it into quarters, and add only 2 teaspoons sugar to each drink.*

Select 4 old-fashioned or short glasses. Put 1 lemon quarter and 1 tablespoon of the sugar in each glass. Muddle well with a muddler or the handle of a wooden spoon. Add 60 ml (2 fl oz) of the *cachaça* to each glass, stir well, and then fill the glasses with ice. Garnish each glass with a lemon slice and serve at once.

Serves 4

1 lemon, cut into quarters

4 tablespoons superfine (caster) sugar

250 ml (8 fl oz) *cachaça*

Ice cubes

4 lemon slices for garnish

Sangria

750 ml (24 fl oz) dry red wine

750 ml (24 fl oz) dry ginger ale

750 ml (24 fl oz) fresh orange juice

1 orange, thinly sliced crosswise

1 lemon, thinly sliced crosswise

Ice cubes

For a stronger drink, use only 250 ml (8 fl oz) ginger ale and add 250 ml (8 fl oz) each brandy and triple sec.

In a punch bowl or pitcher, combine the wine, ginger ale, and orange juice and stir to mix. Add the citrus slices and ice and stir again. Let guests serve themselves.

Serves 4

White Wine Sangria

500 ml (16 fl oz) fresh orange juice

250 ml (8 fl oz) Cointreau or triple sec

2 tablespoons fresh lemon juice

2 tablespoons superfine (caster) sugar

750 ml (24 fl oz) dry white wine

750 ml (24 fl oz) bitter lemon or sparkling water

2 *each* ripe peaches and nectarines, halved, pitted, and thinly sliced

1 lemon, thinly sliced crosswise

Ice cubes

Two of summer's favourite stone fruits, peaches and nectarines, add their natural sweetness to this light and refreshing orange-scented sangria.

In a punch bowl or pitcher, combine the orange juice, Cointreau, lemon juice, and sugar and stir to dissolve the sugar. Pour in the wine and bitter lemon, add all of the sliced fruit and the ice, and stir again. Let guests serve themselves.

Serves 4

Sparkling Wine Sangria

250 ml (8 fl oz) framboise

2 tablespoons fresh lemon juice

2 tablespoons superfine (caster) sugar

750 ml (24 fl oz) cranberry juice

750 ml (24 fl oz) sparkling wine

750 ml (24 fl oz) sparkling water

250 g (8 oz) sliced strawberries

250 g (8 oz) *each* raspberries and blueberries

1 lemon, thinly sliced crosswise

Ice cubes

You can use any high-quality sparkling wine for this berry-rich sangria, such as French Champagne, Spanish Cava, Italian Prosecco, or a California sparkler based on Chardonnay or Pinot Noir grapes.

In a punch bowl or pitcher, combine the framboise, lemon juice, and sugar and stir to dissolve the sugar. Pour in the cranberry juice, sparkling wine, and sparkling water. Add all of the berries, the lemon slices, and the ice and stir again. Let guests serve themselves.

Serves 4

Peach Bellini

Fresh white peaches are traditionally used for making this classic Italian drink. If they are unavailable, purchase white peach purée (either frozen or aseptic packaged) or substitute yellow peaches, which will yield a sweeter flavour and darker colour.

Select 4 Champagne flutes. In a blender, purée the peaches until completely smooth. Taste and add the sugar if needed. Fill each flute about one-third full of the purée. Top with the sparkling wine. Serve at once.

Serves 4

2 ripe peaches, preferably white, peeled, halved, and pitted

About 1 tablespoon superfine (caster) sugar, if needed

1 bottle (750 ml/24 fl oz) Champagne, Prosecco, or sparkling wine, chilled

Figs Wrapped in Prosciutto

Late summer is the season for fresh figs. In this simple preparation, the sugar-sweet flavour of the fruit is contrasted with the mild saltiness of prosciutto. For an alternative presentation, make a lengthwise cut in each whole fig and tuck a strip of prosciutto into the slit. The figs can be assembled up to 6 hours in advance and refrigerated.

Using a sharp knife, cut the prosciutto slices lengthwise into strips 2.5 cm (1 inch) wide. Trim off the tough stem end of the figs and cut each fig in half lengthwise. Wrap each fig half with a strip of prosciutto and place, cut side up, on a tray or platter. If not serving right away, cover with cling film and refrigerate. Bring to room temperature before serving.

Serves 12-14

250 g (1/2 lb) thinly sliced prosciutto

18-24 soft, ripe figs, 750 g-1 kg (11/2-2 lb) total weight

Bite-Sized Courgette Frittata

Frittatas are quick and easy to assemble and cook and can be served at room temperature, making them ideal cocktail-party fare. This recipe calls for courgette, but you can use 155 g (5 oz) chopped cooked asparagus in its place.

2 courgettes

6 large eggs

2 tablespoons single cream

30 g (1 oz) grated Parmesan cheese

3/4 teaspoon salt

1/2 teaspoon freshly ground pepper

2 tablespoons unsalted butter

1 tablespoon extra-virgin olive oil

2 tablespoons finely chopped yellow onion

1 clove garlic, minced

1 teaspoon chopped fresh thyme

10 g (1/3 oz) chopped fresh flat-leaf (Italian) parsley, plus extra for garnish

Using the large holes of a box grater, grate the courgette. Lay the grated courgette on paper towels to drain briefly.

In a large bowl, whisk together the eggs, cream, cheese, salt, and pepper just until blended. Stir in the drained courgette.

Preheat the grill. In a flameproof 25 cm (10 inch) frying pan over medium-high heat, melt the butter with the olive oil. When the butter foams, add the onion and sauté until translucent, 2-3 minutes. Add the garlic, the thyme, and the 10 g (1/3 oz) parsley and sauté for 1 minute longer.

Pour in the egg mixture, reduce the heat to low, and cook until the eggs are just firm around the edges, 3-4 minutes. Using a spatula, lift the edges and tilt the pan to let the uncooked portion flow underneath. Continue cooking until the eggs are nearly set, 4-5 minutes longer.

Slip the pan under the grill about 10 cm (4 inches) from the heat source and grill until the top sets and browns lightly, about 2 minutes. Remove from the grill and slide onto a cutting board; allow to cool. Cut into 2.5 cm (1 inch) pieces. Garnish with the parsley and serve at room temperature.

Serves 12-14

Beef Tenderloin Canapés with Chopped Vine Tomatoes

Few cuts of beef are as succulent as beef tenderloin, which, when thinly sliced, makes an elegant canapé. Here, in the spirit of summer, the slices are given a topping of chopped vine tomatoes, but a dab of prepared horseradish would be delicious, too.

Preheat the oven to 180°C (350°F). Arrange the baguette slices in a single layer on a rimmed baking sheet. Bake until lightly golden, about 15 minutes. Turn the slices over and bake until the second side is lightly golden, about 10 minutes longer. Remove from the oven and set aside. Raise the oven temperature to 230°C (450°F).

In a small bowl, whisk together 2 tablespoons of the olive oil, 1½ teaspoons of the salt, and 1 teaspoon of the pepper. Brush the oil mixture on all sides of the tenderloin and place the tenderloin on a rack in a shallow roasting pan just large enough to accommodate it.

Roast until an instant-read thermometer inserted into the thickest part of the fillet registers 49°C (120°F) for rare, about 20 minutes; 54°C (130°F) for medium-rare, about 25 minutes; or 60°C (140°F) for medium, about 30 minutes. Transfer the beef to a cutting board, cover loosely with aluminium foil, and let rest for 15-20 minutes. Carve against the grain into thin slices.

Chop the tomatoes and place them in a colander to drain for 10 minutes. Sort through the basil leaves and set aside 30 small whole leaves. Using a sharp knife, cut the remaining basil leaves into thin strips.

In a large bowl, combine the remaining 2 tablespoons olive oil, 1 teaspoon salt, and ½ teaspoon pepper. Add the tomatoes and sliced basil and turn gently to coat the tomatoes evenly.

To assemble, place a slice or two of beef on a toasted baguette slice and top with a teaspoon of tomatoes and a basil leaf. To serve, arrange on a platter and garnish with the basil sprigs.

Serves 12-14

30 baguettes slices, 6 mm (¼ inch) thick (about 1 large baguette)

4 tablespoons, (60 ml/2 fl oz) extra-virgin olive oil

2½ teaspoons salt

1½ teaspoons freshly ground pepper

750 g-1 kg (1½-2 lb) piece beef tenderloin, trimmed of fat and sinew

750 g (1½ lb) mixed vine tomatoes

60 g (2 oz) fresh basil leaves, plus sprigs for garnish

White and Yellow Corn Fritters with Romesco Sauce

If you are not too rushed at party time, serve these bite-sized fritters hot out of the frying pan. Otherwise, they are still delicious at room temperature. Guacamole is a good substitute for the romesco *sauce. The sauce can be refrigerated in an airtight container for up to 1 week.*

To make the *romesco* sauce, preheat the oven to 165°C (325°F). Cut off the upper one-third of the garlic bulb and discard. Core the tomatoes. Put the garlic, tomatoes, and red pepper in a baking dish just large enough to hold them and drizzle with the olive oil. Roast, uncovered, until the pepper and tomatoes collapse and the garlic cloves are tender, 30-45 minutes. Remove from the oven and let cool.

Peel the tomatoes. Squeeze the garlic pulp from its papery sheaths. Halve and seed the red pepper. In a food processor, combine the tomatoes, garlic pulp, red pepper, almonds, paprika, vinegar, bread, the 1 teaspoon salt, and the ¼ teaspoon cayenne pepper and process until puréed. Taste and add more salt and cayenne pepper, if desired. Transfer to a bowl, cover, and refrigerate until serving.

To make the fritters, one at a time, hold a cob of corn upright, stem end down, in a shallow dish. Using a sharp knife, slice straight down between the kernels and the cob to remove the kernels, rotating the cob a quarter turn after each cut.

In a large bowl, combine the spring onions, flour, baking powder, salt, and pepper and stir to mix well. Add the egg, milk, and corn kernels and stir just to combine.

In large frying pan over medium-high heat, warm 2 tablespoons of the oil. When the oil is hot, drop in a heaped tablespoonful of the fritter batter, then press down to flatten. Repeat to form more fritters, being careful not to crowd the pan. Cook until golden on the first side, about 3 minutes. Turn over and cook until the second side is golden, about 2 minutes longer. Using a slotted spoon, transfer to paper towels to drain. Repeat with the remaining batter, adding more oil to the pan as needed for each batch.

Place the bowl of *romesco* sauce in the centre of a platter and surround with the fritters. Serve warm or at room temperature.

Serves 12-14

ROMESCO SAUCE

1 bulb garlic

3 large tomatoes

1 red pepper (capsicum)

1 tablespoon extra-virgin olive oil

60 g (2 oz) blanched almonds, toasted

1 teaspoon sweet paprika

2 tablespoons sherry vinegar

3 slices day-old baguette or coarse white bread, crusts removed, cut into 12 mm (½ inch) cubes

1 teaspoon salt, plus more to taste

¼ teaspoon cayenne pepper, plus more to taste

FRITTERS

3 yellow or white cobs of corn, or a mixture, peeled

10 spring onions, including pale green tops, minced

155 g (5 oz) plain flour

1½ teaspoons baking powder

1 teaspoon salt

1 teaspoon freshly ground pepper

1 large egg, lightly beaten

160 ml (5 fl oz) whole milk

90 ml (3 fl oz) rape seed, grape seed, or sunflower oil

FOLD-UP BLUEBERRY AND RASPBERRY FRUIT TARTS

2 packs store-bought shortcrust pastry
dough, each about 33 cm (13 inches)
in diameter and 6 mm (1/4 inch) thick,
thawed in the refrigerator

185 g (6 oz) blueberries

185 g (6 oz) raspberries

90 g (3 oz) sugar

2 teaspoons fresh lemon juice

2 tablespoons cold unsalted butter, cut
into small pieces

*These rustic fruit tarts are sublime when berries are at their seasonal
peak. Or, you can substitute 560 g (18 oz) thinly sliced peaches,
nectarines, or plums, or a mixture, keeping in mind complementary
flavours and colours.*

Preheat the oven to 190°C (375°F). Have ready 2 ungreased rimmed baking sheets.

Place 1 pastry round on a baking sheet. In a large bowl, combine the blueberries, raspberries, sugar, and lemon juice and stir carefully to mix. Place half of the fruit in the centre of the pastry round and gently spread to within 5 cm (2 inches) of the edge. Dot the fruit with half of the butter. Fold the uncovered edges of the pastry over the fruit, covering as much of the fruit as possible and pleating, pinching, and folding the pastry as necessary. Repeat with the second baking sheet and pastry round and the remaining fruit and butter.

Bake until the pastry is golden brown and the fruit is bubbling, about 30 minutes. Let cool on the pans on wire racks for 10-15 minutes. Cut into wedges and serve.

Serves 12-14

WINE & CHEESE PARTY

WORK PLAN

UP TO 6 HOURS IN ADVANCE

stuff the dates

UP TO 2 HOURS IN ADVANCE

make the Cheddar cheese bites

place wines in the refrigerator to chill

bring cheeses to room temperature

JUST BEFORE SERVING

assemble the cheese platters

prepare the cocktails

HOSTING AND SERVING TIPS

- Decorate serving trays and platters with grape leaves and clusters, fig leaves, or olive branches.

- Visit a good cheese store a few days before the party to taste a variety of hard and soft cheeses, then make your choices.

- Ask a trusted wine merchant for red, white, and dessert wine recommendations to pair with your cheeses.

- Set out the cheeses, on a marble slab or cutting board covered with a dome or kitchen towel, a few hours before the party so they come to room temperature.

- Put cut flowers in wine carafes of varying sizes to extend the wine theme.

DRINKS

White Grape Splash

Kir

FOOD

Cheddar Cheese and Sesame Bites

*Dates Stuffed with Parmesan
Slivers and Walnuts*

Wine & Cheese Pairings

snip two kinds of non-toxic foliage, such as citrus leaves for white-wine glasses and small olive branches for red-wine glasses.

cut out a leaf or other shape from a piece of cream-coloured card stock or heavy natural-fibre paper. Write a guest's name on each tag and make a hole in the tag with a hole punch.

tie a piece of foliage and a single tag to each glass with a length of raffia or twine.

write out the suggested cheeses to pair with each wine on a tag, and use raffia or twine to tie it along with a piece of foliage to the appropriate carafe or wine bottle.

Customising Glasses & Carafes

When you are hosting a wine and cheese party, it is a good idea to help your guests both keep track of their wineglasses – red and white – and choose which cheeses to pair with which wines. These simple glass and carafe labels do the job and add an appealing homespun touch.

White Grape Splash

The grapes at the bottom of the glass provide a surprise element and the bright green mint adds a splash of colour to this refreshing drink.

Select 4 tumblers or wineglasses. Put several ice cubes and 6 frozen grapes in each glass. Pour 180 ml (6 fl oz) of the grape juice over the ice, then top with about 60 ml (2 fl oz) of the sparkling water. Garnish each glass with a mint sprig and serve at once.

Serves 4

Ice cubes

2 or 3 bunches red or white grapes, frozen

750 ml (24 fl oz) white grape juice

1 bottle (750 ml/24 fl oz) sparkling water

Fresh mint sprigs for garnish

Kir

Crème de cassis, a liqueur made from blackcurrants, originated in the French city of Dijon. Complement it with a dry white wine to make this classic Gallic aperitif.

Chill 4 tumblers or wineglasses. Pour 2 teaspoons of the crème de cassis into each glass and top with about 160 ml (5 fl oz) of the wine. Garnish with a lemon twist and serve at once.

Serves 4

8 teaspoons crème de cassis

625 ml (20 fl oz) dry white wine such as Sauvignon Blanc, chilled

4 long, narrow lemon twists for garnish

Cheddar Cheese and Sesame Bites

These flavourful mouthfuls can be completely assembled up to 2 hours in advance, then covered and refrigerated, making them a perfect menu item for the host busy with last-minute party details. You can replace the sesame seeds with finely chopped toasted pecans or almonds.

315 g (10 oz) white Cheddar cheese, grated

2 tablespoons sour cream

2 tablespoons unsalted butter, at room temperature

2 tablespoons minced shallot

1/2 teaspoon salt

75 g (2 1/2 oz) sesame seeds, toasted

Line a tray with aluminium foil. In a food processor, combine the cheese, sour cream, butter, shallot, and salt and process until smooth, about 1 minute. Scoop up 1 heaped teaspoon of the mixture, roll between your palms to form a bite-sized ball, and place on the tray. Repeat with the remaining mixture. Refrigerate the balls until firm, about 1 hour.

Spread the sesame seeds on a plate. Roll the balls in the seeds, coating them evenly. Once the balls are coated, sprinkle any remaining seeds on a platter. Rest the balls on the seeds and serve.

Serves 8-10

Dates Stuffed with Parmesan Slivers and Walnuts

Sweet dates pair beautifully with salty Parmesan, while the walnuts add an earthy taste and a crunchy texture. Medjool dates are rich and meaty, making them perfect for stuffing. You can stone the dates in advance and assemble the appetizer up to 6 hours before serving.

24 large dates, preferably Medjool

60 g (2 oz) piece Parmesan cheese

24 walnut halves

With a paring knife, make a small lengthwise incision in each date and carefully remove the stones.

Using a vegetable peeler, shave the cheese into ribbons. Tuck some cheese and a walnut half into the slit in each date. Arrange on a platter and serve.

Serves 8-10

RED WINE
CHEESE PLAT

RED WINE PAIRINGS

The rich, full flavour of red wine pairs handsomely with complex cheeses, apples, and grapes. Toasted walnuts contribute a hint of smokiness, while the honeycomb lends a welcome sweetness.

About 2 hours before serving, remove the cheeses from the refrigerator, unwrap them, and allow them to come to room temperature.

When ready to serve, arrange the cheeses, apple slices, grapes, toasted walnuts, and honeycomb on a cutting board, marble slab, or 1 or more platters.

Serves 8-10

250-315 g (8-10 oz) Brie cheese

250-315 g (8-10 oz) Cheddar cheese

250-315 g (8-10 oz) Spanish drunken goat cheese

1 apple, thinly sliced

2 small bunches grapes, 1 red and 1 white

60 g (2 oz) walnuts, toasted

185 g (6 oz) honeycomb

PAIRING RED WINE WITH CHEESE

Pair big-flavoured, full-bodied wines — such as Bordeaux, Sangiovese, or Syrah — with tangy, soft-ripened cheeses, such as Brie or Camembert.

Pair spicy, full-bodied wines — such as Cabernet Sauvignon, Rioja, or Zinfandel — with sharp, salty cheeses, such as Cheddar, pecorino, Parmigiano-Reggiano, or Asiago.

Pair fruity, medium-bodied wines — such as Pinot Noir or Barbera — with semisoft, mild goat cheeses, such as Spanish drunken goat, *Crottin de Chavignol*, or *Selles-sur-Cher*.

250-315 g (8-10 oz) Beaufort
cheese

250-315 g (8-10 oz) herbed goat
cheese

250-315 g (8-10 oz) Manchego
cheese

1 small jar chutney

60 g (2 oz) almonds, toasted

250 g (½ lb) dried figs

WHITE WINE PAIRINGS

The crisp, citrus flavours of white wine pair equally well with cheeses that range from buttery Beaufort to tangy herbed goat cheese. A good quality chutney adds a sweet-and-sour note that blends with the cheeses, as do the salty nuts and dried fruit.

About 2 hours before serving, remove the cheeses from the refrigerator, unwrap them, and allow them to come to room temperature.

When ready to serve, arrange the cheeses, chutney, toasted almonds, and dried figs on a cutting board, marble slab, or 1 or more platters.

Serves 8-10

PAIRING WHITE WINE WITH CHEESE

Pair full-bodied wines — such as Chardonnay — with mild, creamy cheeses, such as Beaufort or Gruyère.

Pair light, fruity wines — such as Sauvignon Blanc or Pinot Gris — with tangy herbed or plain fresh goat cheeses.

Pair crisp, spicy wines — such as Gewürztraminer or Riesling — with salty, aged cheeses, such as Manchego or pecorino.

Dessert Wine Pairings

Cheeses with bold flavours, such as Gorgonzola and Stilton, are ideal for pairing with rich dessert wines that will complement their strong flavours, rather than be overwhelmed by them. Some pear slices and a handful of toasted pecans round out the platter.

About 2 hours before serving, remove the cheeses from the refrigerator, unwrap them, and allow them to come to room temperature.

When ready to serve, arrange the cheeses, pear slices, and toasted pecans on a marble slab, cutting board, or 1 or more platters.

Serves 8-10

250-315 g (8-10 oz) Gorgonzola cheese

250-315 g (8-10 oz) Stilton cheese

250-315 g (8-10 oz) Muenster cheese

1 pear, thinly sliced

60 g (2 oz) pecans, toasted

PAIRING DESSERT WINE WITH CHEESE

Pair sweet fortified wines — such as Port, sherry, or Madeira — with pungent blue cheeses, such as Gorgonzola, Stilton, or Spanish Cabrales.

Pair sweet white wines — such as Sauternes or late-harvest Riesling — with soft, creamy cheeses, such as Muenster or Taleggio.

WINTER COCKTAILS

WORK PLAN

UP TO 2 DAYS IN ADVANCE

prepare the chicken liver mousse

UP TO 12 HOURS IN ADVANCE

bake the tartlet shells

UP TO 8 HOURS IN ADVANCE

bake the profiteroles

prepare the caviar dip

JUST BEFORE SERVING

prepare the fondue

make the toast triangles

prepare the oysters

assemble the tartlets and
the profiteroles

mix the cocktails

HOSTING AND
SERVING TIPS

- Light a fire in the fireplace just before the guests arrive and have extra logs on hand. Recruit a guest to tend the fire throughout the party.

- Use a variety of candles in different kinds of candleholders, and dim the lights to create a cosy atmosphere.

- Place platters of appetisers on tables throughout the room, so guests can mingle near the hearth.

- Set out stacks of cocktail napkins at each food station.

- Offer a special non-alcoholic mixed drink along with elegant cocktails.

- Have trays set up in advance with everything you will need to serve coffee and tea with dessert.

DRINKS

Pomegranate Sparklers

Champagne with Liqueurs

Classic Martinis

Vodka Metropolitans

FOOD

Oysters Rockefeller

Chicken Liver Mousse with Cornichons

Caviar Dip with Toast Triangles

Cheese Fondue

Mini Profiteroles

Lemon Curd Tartlets

SETTING UP A HOME BAR

For intimate gatherings, set up a cocktail and Champagne bar right in the party room. All you need is a small space, such as a shelf or side table. Group ice, glassware, spirits, and garnishes in a logical flow to facilitate drink making. Practice mixing drinks in advance to get the setup right. Chill glasses by filling with ice (discard before using) or placing in the freezer for 15-30 minutes.

cover a flat surface with a runner or mats to absorb spills and to tie the look together. Arrange glassware by type so that it is easy to select what you need quickly.

organise bar tools, including a cocktail shaker, strainer, ice bucket, mixing spoons, and measuring devices. Place Champagne in a cooler or ice bucket to chill.

arrange matching bowls of garnishes such as pimiento-stuffed olives, citrus twists, and capers on the bar. Leave ample space for drink mixing.

POMEGRANATE SPARKLERS

A number of the pomegranate syrups now on the market are not as sweet as grenadine, the best-known pomegranate syrup. If you cannot find one of them, use grenadine but increase the amount of lime juice in each drink to 80 ml (3 fl oz).

Chill 4 martini or cocktail glasses. Fill a tall cocktail shaker half full with ice. Add 60 ml (2 fl oz) each of the pomegranate syrup and lime juice. Cover and shake for 20 seconds. Strain into a glass and top with sparkling water. Repeat to fill 3 more glasses. Garnish each glass with a lime slice and a sprinkling of pomegranate seeds. Serve at once.

Serves 4

Ice cubes

250 ml (8 fl oz) pomegranate syrup

250 ml (8 fl oz) fresh lime juice
(8-10 limes)

1 bottle (750 ml/24 fl oz) sparkling water

Thin lime slices for garnish

Pomegranate seeds for garnish

CHAMPAGNE WITH LIQUEURS

Few drinks are more elegant or appreciated than Champagne. Adding crème de cassis to it creates the famous Kir royale. Whichever liqueur you choose, add only a small amount for a hint of flavour, or you will diminish the taste of the Champagne.

Select 4 Champagne flutes. Pour 1 tablespoon of the desired liqueur into each glass. Top with about 125 ml (4 fl oz) of the Champagne. Stir and serve at once.

Serves 4

60 ml (2 fl oz) framboise, crème de cassis, or amaretto

1 bottle (750 ml/24 fl oz) Champagne or other sparkling wine, chilled

CLASSIC MARTINIS

Aficionados of the martini argue over how dry it should be, a quality controlled by the amount of vermouth. For a dry martini, reduce the amount of vermouth by half. For an even drier version, reduce it to a few drops. You can vary the garnish, too, trading out the olive for a caper, or for a cocktail onion, which turns the martini into a Gibson.

Chill 4 martini glasses. Fill a tall cocktail shaker half full with ice. Pour in the gin and vermouth. Stir or cover with the lid and shake for 20 seconds. Strain into the chilled glasses. Garnish each glass with an olive or two on a cocktail stick.

Serves 4

Ice cubes

430 ml (14 fl oz) gin

60 ml (2 fl oz) dry vermouth

4-8 green olives for garnish

VODKA METROPOLITANS

The classic metropolitan is made with brandy, sweet vermouth, sugar, and bitters, with the vermouth giving the popular cocktail a lovely red tint. In this version, made with blackcurrant-infused vodka, cranberry juice delivers the rosy colour.

Chill 4 martini glasses. Fill a tall cocktail shaker half full with ice. Pour in the vodka, lime juice, and cranberry juice. Cover with the lid and shake for 20 seconds. Strain into the chilled glasses and garnish each with a lime wedge. Serve at once.

Serves 4

Ice cubes

310 ml (10 fl oz) blackcurrant-infused vodka

125 ml (4 fl oz) fresh lime juice

60 ml (2 fl oz) cranberry juice

4 lime wedges for garnish

OYSTERS ROCKEFELLER

Oysters Rockefeller, created in New Orleans at the famed Antoine's Restaurant and named because the rich spinach mixture topping each oyster is the colour of a dollar bill, are elegant, easy to eat, and delicious. Make sure the rock salt is deep enough to hold the oyster shells upright, so neither the liquor nor the topping spills during cooking.

Rock salt

24 medium-sized oysters

330 g (10^1/$_2$ oz) well-drained cooked spinach

4 spring onions, including pale green tops, chopped

15 g (^{1}/$_2$ oz) store-bought or freshly made bread crumbs

6 fresh flat-leaf (Italian) parsley sprigs, coarsely chopped

^{1}/$_2$ teaspoon salt

^{1}/$_4$ teaspoon freshly ground pepper

4 tablespoons (60 g/2 oz) unsalted butter, at room temperature

2 tablespoons Pernod or other anise liqueur

2 or 3 drops Tabasco sauce or other hot-pepper sauce (optional)

Preheat the grill. Fill 4 pie dishes with rock salt 12 mm (^{1}/$_2$ inch) deep.

Scrub the oysters well, then rinse under running cold water. Discard any oysters that don't close to the touch. Working with 1 oyster at a time, use a thick folded towel or cloth to hold the oyster in one hand, with the flat top shell facing up. Using an oyster knife in the other hand, insert its tip between the shells near the hinge of the oyster. Carefully twist the knife – it may take a bit of strength – to break the hinge. Run the knife along the inside surface of the top shell to loosen the oyster from it. Lift off and discard the top shell. Run the knife along the inside surface of the bottom shell to sever the muscle that attaches the shell to the oyster. As the oysters are opened, nest them in the pie pans, putting 6 oysters in each pan.

In a food processor, combine the spinach, spring onions, bread crumbs, parsley, salt, and pepper and pulse just until mixed. Add the butter, the Pernod, and the Tabasco sauce, if using, and process until smooth. Taste and adjust the seasoning. Spoon an equal amount of the spinach mixture on top of each oyster. Slip 2 pie dishes under the grill 10 cm (4 inches) from the heat source and grill until the spinach mixture is lightly browned and bubbling and the edges of the oysters are curled, about 8 minutes. Serve at once. Repeat with the remaining oysters.

Serves 12-14

CHICKEN LIVER MOUSSE WITH CORNICHONS

Simple yet sophisticated, chicken liver mousse goes together quickly and can be made up to 2 days in advance of the party, covered, and refrigerated. Just a quick stir is all that it needs before serving. For a richer mousse, substitute duck livers for the chicken livers.

In a frying pan over medium heat, melt 45 g (1½ oz) of the butter. When it foams, add the chicken livers and pepper and cook, stirring occasionally, until the livers are firm but still rosy inside, about 10 minutes. Remove the pan from the heat and pour in the warmed brandy. Light a long match and carefully hold it just above the pan, igniting the fumes. Return the pan to medium-high heat. Stir the livers and shake the pan slowly until most of the alcohol evaporates, about 1 minute. Transfer to a food processor.

In the same pan over medium-low heat, melt the remaining 45 g (1½ oz) butter. When it foams, add the shallots, apple, and thyme and cook, stirring occasionally, until the apple pieces are soft, about 20 minutes. Transfer to the food processor and let cool. Process until smooth. Add the 125 g (4 oz) butter and the cream and process until a smooth purée forms.

Spoon the mousse into a ramekin just large enough to hold it and smooth the surface. Cover the ramekin and refrigerate for several hours until the mousse is firm.

To serve, stir the mousse briefly and then spread a small amount on each water biscuit. Top each biscuit with 2 gherkin slivers and serve.

Serves 12-14

90 g (3 oz) plus 125 g (4 oz) unsalted butter, at room temperature

500 g (1 lb) chicken livers, membranes removed and any soft or discoloured spots trimmed

¼ teaspoon freshly ground pepper

80 ml (3 fl oz) brandy, warmed

45 g (1½ oz) coarsely chopped shallots

1 tart apple such as Granny Smith, peeled, cored, and coarsely chopped

1 teaspoon fresh thyme leaves

90 ml (3 fl oz) double cream

36 water biscuits

8-10 pickled gherkins, cut lengthwise into thin slivers

CAVIAR DIP WITH TOAST TRIANGLES

Although black caviar is suggested here, golden caviar or salmon roe make eye-catching substitutions.

Preheat the oven to 180°C (350°F). Arrange the triangles in a single layer on a rimmed baking sheet. Bake until lightly golden, about 15 minutes. Turn the triangles and bake until the second side is lightly golden, about 10 minutes longer. Remove from the oven, allow to cool, and set aside.

Finely chop the eggs. In a small bowl, mix together the eggs, shallots, crème fraîche, cream, salt and pepper to taste. Spread the mixture in a layer 12 mm ($^1/_2$ inch) deep in a bowl about 20 cm (8 inches) in diameter and 2.5 cm (1 inch) deep.

Spoon a thin, even layer of caviar along one side of a dinner knife. Gently push the caviar onto the egg mixture, making a strip the width of the dinner knife and reaching from one side of the bowl to the other. Repeat, spacing the strips 6 mm ($^1/_4$ inch) apart, until you have used all the caviar. Sprinkle the dip with the chives and serve with the toast triangles.

12 thin slices white sandwich bread, crusts removed, each slice cut into 4 triangles

4 large eggs, hard boiled and shelled

45 g (1$^1/_2$ oz) minced shallots

60 g (2 oz) crème fraîche

2 tablespoons double cream

Salt and freshly ground pepper

45-60 g (1$^1/_2$-2 oz) black caviar

1 tablespoon minced fresh chives

CHEESE FONDUE

Cheese fondue is traditionally served in a special ceramic pot that fits on the burner, but you can substitute a metal fondue pot, using it for both cooking and serving the fondue.

Preheat the oven to 120°C (250°F). Place a ceramic fondue pot in the oven. In a small bowl, stir together the cornflour and kirsch until smooth. Set aside.

In a heavy saucepan over high heat, combine the garlic and wine. When bubbles form around the edges, reduce the heat to medium-low and add the cheeses, little by little, stirring constantly with a wooden spoon in a zigzag pattern to prevent the cheese from forming clumps. When all of the cheese has been added and has melted, stir in the cornflour mixture, nutmeg, and pepper.

Light the fondue burner and place it on the table. Pour the cheese mixture into the warmed fondue pot and place over the burner. Serve the bread cubes alongside.

Each recipe serves 12-14

2 tablespoons cornflour

2 tablespoons kirsch

6 cloves garlic, crushed

500 ml (16 fl oz) dry white wine such as Sauvignon Blanc

875 g (1$^3/_4$ lb) Gruyère or Beaufort cheese, grated

375 g ($^3/_4$ lb) Emmentaler cheese, grated

1 teaspoon freshly grated nutmeg

$^1/_2$ teaspoon freshly ground pepper

1$^1/_2$ day-old baguettes, cut into 12 mm ($^1/_2$ inch) cubes

MINI PROFITEROLES

Bake these bite-sized profiteroles up to 8 hours in advance and fill with whipped cream just before serving.

Preheat the oven to 220°C (425°F). Line 2 baking sheets with nonstick liners or parchment (baking) paper.

In a saucepan over medium-high heat, combine the water, butter, salt, and granulated sugar and bring to a boil. Cook, stirring constantly with a wooden spoon, until the butter melts, 3-4 minutes. Add the flour and mix vigorously until the dough pulls away from the sides of the pan, about 3 minutes. Remove from the heat, make a well in the centre, add 1 egg to the well, and beat until combined. Repeat with 3 more eggs. Dip a small spoon into cold water, scoop up a generous teaspoon of the dough, and push it onto a baking sheet. Repeat, forming 30 puffs in all. Brush each top with the beaten egg.

Bake for 10 minutes, reduce the oven temperature to 180°C (350°F), and bake until golden brown, about 15 minutes longer. Turn off the oven, pierce the bottom of each puff with a bamboo skewer, and leave in the oven for 10 minutes. Transfer to a wire rack and allow to cool completely. Cut in half horizontally to fill.

Put a heaped spoonful of the whipped cream in the bottom of each pastry and replace the tops. Place on a platter, dust with the icing sugar, and serve.

250 ml (8 fl oz) water

90 g (3 oz) unsalted butter

1 teaspoon salt

1 teaspoon granulated sugar

155 g (5 oz) plain flour

4 large eggs, plus 1 egg, lightly beaten

250 ml (8 fl oz) double cream whipped with 60 g (2 oz) granulated sugar to stiff peaks

3 tablespoons icing sugar

LEMON CURD TARTLETS

Ready-to-roll shortcrust pastry dough and ready-made lemon curd mean that these tartlets go together easily and quickly. Vary the garnishes, if you like.

2 rolls store-bought pie pastry dough, about 33 cm (13 inches) in diameter and 6 mm (1/4 inch) thick, thawed in the refrigerator

845 g (30 oz) store-bought or homemade lemon curd

Whipped cream, fresh mint sprigs, and/or candied violets for garnish (optional)

Preheat the oven to 200°C (400°F). Have ready mini-muffin pans with 24 cups. Using a 5 cm (2 inch) round cutter, cut out 24 pastry rounds. Fit a round into each muffin cup. Make a loose ball of aluminium foil and place into each cup and bake for 4 minutes. Remove the foil, prick each pastry shell with fork tines, and continue to bake until golden, 2-3 minutes longer. Let cool completely on wire racks.

To serve, fill the tartlet shells with the lemon curd and garnish each tartlet with the whipped cream, mint, and/or violets, if desired.

Each recipe serves 12-14

Additional Drink Recipes

The following cocktails can be added to your existing party menu or served alone. Each recipe yields 1 drink but can easily be multiplied according to the number of guests at your party.

Negroni

Ice cubes

2 tablespoons gin

2 tablespoons sweet vermouth

2 tablespoons Campari

Orange slice for garnish

Fill an old-fashioned glass or tumbler with ice. Fill a cocktail shaker half full with ice. Pour in the gin, sweet vermouth, and Campari. Cover with the lid and shake for 20 seconds, then strain into the glass. Garnish with the orange slice.

Makes 1 drink

Manhattan

Ice cubes

5 tablespoons, 75 ml (2¹/₂ fl oz) bourbon

1¹/₂ tablespoons sweet vermouth

1 dash of Angostura bitters

Maraschino cherry and orange peel strip for garnish

Chill a cocktail glass. Fill a cocktail shaker half full with ice. Pour in the bourbon, vermouth, and bitters. Cover with the lid and shake for 20 seconds, then strain into the glass. Garnish with the cherry and orange peel strip.

Makes 1 drink

Sidecar

Ice cubes

5 tablespoons (75 ml/2¹/₂ fl oz) brandy

1 tablespoon triple sec

1 tablespoon fresh lemon juice

Lemon peel strip for garnish

Chill a cocktail glass. Fill a cocktail shaker half full with ice. Pour in the brandy, triple sec, and lemon juice. Cover with the lid and shake for 20 seconds, then strain into the glass. Tie the lemon peel strip into a knot and garnish the drink.

Makes 1 drink

Venetian Sunset

Ice cubes

3 tablespoons gin

1 tablespoon dry vermouth

1 tablespoon Campari

1 tablespoon Grand Marnier

Orange twist for garnish

Chill a cocktail glass. Fill a cocktail shaker half full with ice. Pour in the gin, vermouth, Campari, and Grand Marnier. Cover with the lid and shake for 20 seconds, then strain into the glass. Garnish with the orange twist.

Makes 1 drink

Balsamic Bloody Mary

Ice cubes

125 ml (4 fl oz) tomato juice

60 ml (2 fl oz) vodka

1 tablespoon fresh lime juice

1 teaspoon balsamic vinegar

2 dashes of Worcestershire sauce

2 dashes of Tabasco sauce

1/4 teaspoon freshly ground pepper

1/4 teaspoon salt

1/4 teaspoon ground cumin

Lime wedge and celery stalk for garnish

Fill a tall glass with ice. Fill a cocktail shaker half full with ice. Add the tomato juice, vodka, lime juice, balsamic vinegar, Worcestershire sauce, Tabasco sauce, pepper, salt, and cumin. Cover and shake for 20 seconds, then strain into the glass. Garnish with the lime wedge and celery stalk.

Makes 1 drink

COCKTAIL CALCULATOR

Here are basic guidelines for planning the number of drinks to serve at a typical 2^1/$_2$-hour cocktail party. Adjust up or down depending on the weather, age of guests, time of day, and amount of food being served.

Cocktails 2^1/$_2$ per person

Champagne or sparkling wine 1 bottle for every 2 to 3 guests

Wine 1 bottle for every 2 to 3 guests

Liquor 1 litre for every 10 to 12 guests

Filtered water 1 litre for every 2 guests

SIMPLE SYRUP

Bartenders usually have a bottle of this syrup on hand for sweetening cocktails. This recipe can be made ahead of time and stored in the refrigerator for up to 2 months.

In a large saucepan over medium-high heat, bring 250 ml (8 fl oz) water to a simmer. Add 250 g (8 oz) sugar and stir until completely dissolved. Remove from the heat and set aside to cool to room temperature. Pour the syrup into a clean bottle, cap, and refrigerate until needed.

Makes 375 ml (12 fl oz)

TOM COLLINS

Ice cubes

60 ml (2 fl oz) gin

1 tablespoon fresh lemon juice

1 tablespoon simple syrup (recipe above)

160-180 ml (5-6 fl oz) sparkling water

Lemon wedge for garnish

Fill a Collins or tall glass with ice. Fill a cocktail shaker half full with ice. Pour in the gin, lemon juice, and simple syrup. Cover with the lid and shake for 20 seconds, then strain into the glass. Top with the sparkling water. Stir and garnish with the lemon wedge.

Makes 1 drink

SAZERAC

1/2 teaspoon Pernod or Ricard

Ice cubes

60 ml (2 fl oz) rye whiskey or bourbon

1 tablespoon simple syrup (recipe above)

2 dashes of Peychaud (or Angostura) bitters

Lemon twist for garnish

Chill an old-fashioned glass or tumbler. Coat the interior of the glass with the Pernod. Fill a cocktail shaker two-thirds full with ice. Add the whiskey, simple syrup, and bitters and stir well. Strain into the chilled glass. Garnish with the lemon twist.

Makes 1 drink

RUM COLLINS

Ice cubes

60 ml (2 fl oz) dark rum

1 tablespoon fresh lemon juice

1 tablespoon simple syrup (recipe above)

160-180 ml (5-6 fl oz) sparkling water

Lemon wedge and maraschino cherry for garnish

Fill a Collins or tall glass with ice. Fill a cocktail shaker half full with ice. Pour in the rum, lemon juice, and simple syrup. Cover with the lid and shake for 20 seconds, then strain into the glass. Top with the sparkling water. Garnish with the lemon wedge and cherry.

Makes 1 drink

Planter's Punch

Ice cubes

60 ml (2 fl oz) dark rum

60 ml (2 fl oz) fresh grapefruit juice

2 tablespoons pineapple juice

2 tablespoons fresh lime juice

1 tablespoon simple syrup (recipe on page 138)

2 tablespoons sparkling water

Pineapple spear for garnish

Fill a Collins or tall glass with ice. Fill a cocktail shaker half full with ice cubes. Pour in the rum, all the fruit juices, and the simple syrup. Cover with the lid and shake for about 20 seconds, then strain into the glass. Top with the sparkling water. Stir briefly and garnish with the pineapple spear.

Makes 1 drink

Whiskey Sour

Ice cubes

60 ml (2 fl oz) whiskey

1 1/2 tablespoons fresh lemon juice

1 tablespoon simple syrup (recipe on page 138)

Orange slice and maraschino cherry for garnish

Chill a wineglass or tumbler in the freezer. Fill a cocktail shaker two-thirds full with ice. Pour in the whiskey, lemon juice, and simple syrup. Cover with the lid and shake for 20 seconds, then strain into the chilled glass. Garnish with the orange slice and maraschino cherry.

Makes 1 drink

Long Island Iced Tea

Ice cubes

1 tablespoon gin

1 tablespoon light rum

1 tablespoon silver tequila

1 tablespoon vodka

1 tablespoon triple sec

2 tablespoons fresh lemon juice

1 tablespoon simple syrup (recipe on page 138)

160 ml (5 fl oz) cola

Lemon wedge for garnish

Fill a Collins or tall glass with ice. Fill a cocktail shaker half full with ice. Pour in the gin, rum, tequila, vodka, triple sec, lemon juice, and simple syrup. Cover with the lid and shake for 20 seconds, then strain into the glass. Top with the cola and garnish with the lemon wedge.

Makes 1 drink

INDEX

ACKNOWLEDGEMENTS

WELDON OWEN wishes to thank the following individuals for their kind assistance: Lisa Atwood, Carrie Bradley, Patrick Coghlan, Ken DellaPenta, Peggy Fallon, Dale Hunter, Edward Kavalee, Tippy Kavalee, Jamie Kenyon, Jason Levin, Adam Marshall, Anna Migirova, Susan Morales, Lesli Neilson, Lucie Parker, Jarred Shein, Sharon Silva, Kate Washington, and Heather Wheatland.

GEORGEANNE BRENNAN would like to thank her family and friends for being such enthusiastic research assistants, never failing to taste test a cocktail or appetiser.

BEN MASTERS would like to thank Macleay on Manning and Norton Street Grocer, both in Sydney, Australia.

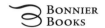

BONNIER BOOKS

Appledram Barns
Birdham Road
Chichester
West Sussex
PO20 7EQ

Bonnier Books Edition
First published 2007

Bonnier Books Website
www.bonnierbooks.co.uk

A WELDON OWEN PRODUCTION

Printed in China

ISBN-13: 978-1-905825-24-0

Jacket Images

Front cover: Classic Cosmopolitans and
Blood Orange Cosmopolitans, page 54.
Back cover: Crostini with Broad Bean Spread and Mint, page 78;
Winter Cocktails, page 118; Pomegranate Sparklers, page 127.

THE ENTERTAINING SERIES

Conceived and produced by Weldon Owen Inc.

814 Montgomery Street, San Francisco, CA 94133

Telephone: 415 291 0100 Fax: 415 291 8841

In Collaboration with Williams-Sonoma, Inc.
3250 Van Ness Avenue, San Francisco, CA 94109

WELDON OWEN INC.

Chief Executive Officer: John Owen

President and Chief Operating Officer: Terry Newell

Chief Financial Officer: Christine E. Munson

Vice President, International Sales: Stuart Laurence

Vice President and Creative Director: Gaye Allen

Vice President and Publisher: Hannah Rahill

Associate Publisher: Amy Marr

Associate Editor: Donita Boles

Art Director: Colin Wheatland

Production Director: Chris Hemesath

Colour Manager: Teri Bell

Co-edition and Reprint Coordinator: Todd Rechner

Assistant Food Stylists: Louise Masters and Zoe Rixon

Photographer's Assistant: David Finato

Assistant Prop Stylist: Brigid Healy